Living on a

Mountain

Heinemann Library
Chicago, Illinois

Carol Baldwin

©2004 Heinemann Library
a division of Reed Elsevier Inc.
Chicago, Illinois

Customer Service 888-454-2279

Visit our website at www.heinemannlibrary.com

Designed by Kimberly Saar, Heinemann Library
Illustrations and maps by John Fleck
Photo research by Alan Gottlieb
Printed and bound in the United States by Lake Book Manufacturing, Inc.

08 07 06 05 04
10 9 8 7 6 5 4 3 2 1

Library of Congress Cataloging-in-Publication Data
Baldwin, Carol.
  Living on a mountain / Carol Baldwin.
    v. cm. -- (Living habitats
Includes bibliographical references and index.
Contents: What are mountains? -- Why are mountains important? -- What's green and growing in the mountains? -- What animals live in the mountains? -- How do animals live in the mountains? -- What's for dinner in the mountains? -- How do mountain animals get food? -- How do mountains affect people? -- How do people affect mountains?
  ISBN 1-4034-2993-6 (Library Binding-hardcover) -- ISBN 1-4034-3233-3 (Paperback)
  1. Mountain ecology--Juvenile literature. [1. Mountains. 2. Mountain ecology. 3. Ecology.] I. Title.
  QH541.5.M65B35 2003
                                577.5'3--dc21

Acknowledgments
The author and publishers are grateful to the following for permission to reproduce copyright material:
p. 4 Sharna Balfour/Gallo Images/Corbis; p. 5 James L. Amos/Corbis; p. 7 Kevin and Betty Collins/Visuals Unlimited; p. 8 Randall J. Hodaes/Bruce Coleman Inc.; p. 9 George Gerster/NMR; p. 10 Hubertus Kanus/Photo Researchers, Inc.; p. 11 Tom Kloster; p. 12 Joy Spurr/Bruce Coleman Inc.; p. 13 Wolfgang Kaehler/Corbis; p. 14 Tom McHugh/Photo Researchers, Inc.; p. 15 Anthony Mercieca Photo/Photo Researchers, Inc.; p. 16 Tom and Pat Leeson/Photo Researchers, Inc.; p. 17 Galen Rowell/Corbis; p. 18 Mark Boulton/Photo Researchers, Inc.; p. 19 Walt Anderson/Visuals Unlimited; p. 20 Craig K. Lorenz/Photo Researchers, Inc.; p. 21 Jeff Lepore/Photo Researchers, Inc.; p. 22 Photo Researchers, Inc.; p. 24 Bruce Coleman Inc.; p. 25 AP/Wide World Photos; p. 26 M.F. Soper/Bruce Coleman Inc.; p. 27 Phil Schermeister/Corbis.

Cover photograph by Tui De Roy/Roving Tortoise Photography

About the cover: The Andean condor is native to South America. It is the largest bird of prey in the world. It has a wingspan of ten feet, stands four feet (1.2 meters) tall, and can weigh 30 pounds (13.6 kilograms).

Some words are shown in bold, **like this**. You can find out what they mean by looking in the glossary.

Contents

1 What Are Mountains?

Bear Mountain in New York is 1,200 feet (366 meters) tall. Mount Everest in Nepal is 29,108 feet (8,872 meters) tall. Both of these are mountains. A mountain is a landform that rises at least 1,000 feet (300 meters) above the surrounding land. Every continent on Earth has mountains.

Mountains form in different ways

Strong movements of the earth under the ground form mountains. The force of these movements pushes rock layers upward. Volcanic mountains form when molten rock forces its way to Earth's surface.

A group of mountains is called a **range.** The Rocky Mountains in North America and the Andes in South America are mountain ranges. So are the Alps in Europe and the Himalayas in Asia.

> Africa's tallest mountain is Mount Kilimanjaro in Tanzania. It is not part of a mountain range. It is a single volcanic mountain.

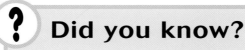

? **Did you know?**
A mountain is measured by its **altitude.** This is how high it is above the ocean or sea level.

The Appalachians were once more than 13,000 feet (3,960 meters) high. But more than 250 million years of **erosion** have worn them down. Now the tallest peak is only 6,684 feet (2,037 meters) high.

Mountains change over time

Most mountains formed millions of years ago. Over time, some mountains get shorter. Ice, wind, and rain wear them down. North America's Appalachians and the Urals in Russia are lower now than they used to be. Volcanic mountains sometimes explode. Mount St. Helens in Washington lost its top and one side this way. Other mountains grow because of movements in Earth's crust. The Himalayas are growing about 3.3 feet (1 meter) every thousand years.

Paricutin

In 1943, a Mexican farmer saw the ground in his cornfield crack open. Smoke and ash started coming from the crack. The ground started to rise. Paricutin volcano was forming. The volcano continued to grow for eight years. It formed a mountain 1,100 feet (336 meters) high the first year. In the next seven years, it grew another 290 feet (88 meters).

Mountains have different life zones

As you travel up a mountain, it gets colder. The temperature drops about 3 °F (1.7 °C) for every 1,000 feet (348 meters) you go up. The air becomes thinner and there is not as much oxygen in it. The wind also blows harder. These changes affect the kinds life found in different areas, or zones, on the same mountain. Most mountains have several **life zones.** Each zone contains different kinds of plants and animals. Only plants and animals **adapted** to the **habitat** can live in each zone. For example, in the Alps of Europe, forests of **broad-leaved** trees grow at the base of mountains. Forests of pines and other **evergreens** grow higher on the mountain where it is colder. Only plants adapted to the cold can grow still higher on the mountain. On the mountain top, there is only snow and bare rock.

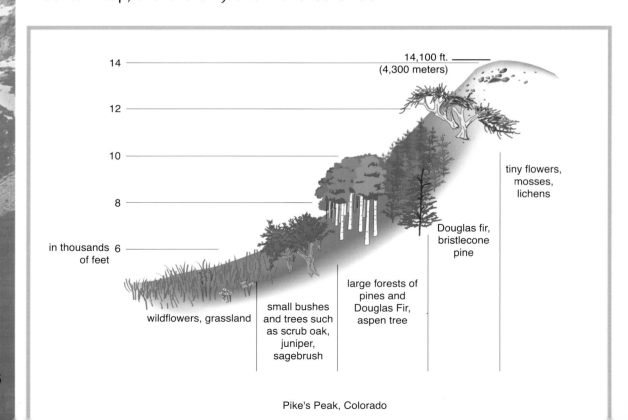

14 ── 14,100 ft. ───
(4,300 meters)

12 ──

10 ──

8 ──

in thousands 6 ──
of feet

tiny flowers, mosses, lichens

Douglas fir, bristlecone pine

large forests of pines and Douglas Fir, aspen tree

wildflowers, grassland

small bushes and trees such as scrub oak, juniper, sagebrush

Pike's Peak, Colorado

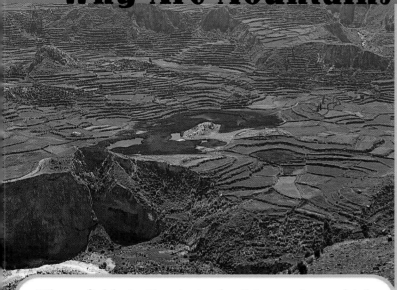

Mountains have many different habitats. This allows many different plants and animals to live on mountains. People live in mountain **ranges** and use the mountains' **resources.**

These fields in Peru's Andes Mountains, which were cut like steps, have been farmed for at least a thousand years.

People live on mountains

Mountains are home to many people. Incas and other Indian cultures have lived in the Andes for thousands of years. Large cities are also found in mountains. Quito, Ecuador, is in the Andes. Bern, Switzerland, is in the Alps. And Denver, Colorado, is in the Rocky Mountains. Because the Himalayas are so high, most people live in valleys between mountain peaks.

Mountains form natural borders

Some mountains separate countries. The Pyrenees separate France and Spain. The Andes separate Chile and Argentina. Others divide continents. The Urals divide Europe from Asia.

 ## Did you know?

La Paz, Bolivia, is the world's highest capital city. It is located nearly 12,000 feet (3,660 meters) high in the Andes Mountains.

7

Mountains affect climate

Mountains can affect the **climates** of lowlands around them. One example is what happens along the west coasts of North and South America. In both places, damp air blows from the Pacific Ocean onto the land. In the northwestern United States, the air runs into the Cascade Mountain **range.** In South America, it runs into the Andes. When the damp air reaches the mountains, it rises and cools. Clouds form and heavy rains fall on the western slopes. Forests can grow here. When the air reaches the mountains' eastern sides, it is dry. Very little rain falls here. This is called the rain shadow effect. Some of Earth's driest deserts are separated from wet forests by only a few hundred miles.

Land to the east of the Cascade Mountains in Washington does not get much rain. So only plants like sagebrush are able to grow there.

Mountains have mineral resources

Mountains have been the source of **minerals** for centuries. Indians of South America mined gold in the Andes for hundreds of years. But now mostly copper and tin are mined in the Andes. Russians mine iron, copper, and zinc in the Ural Mountains. Austrians mine salt in the Alps. Copper, gold, and silver are mined in the Rocky Mountains of North America.

Mountains are home to living things

Because mountains have different **life zones,** they have great **biodiversity.** That means they are home to many different **species** of life. Some of these living things are found nowhere else on Earth.

This salt mine is located in mountains near Nordrhein Westphalia in Germany. It is the largest salt mine in the world.

? **Did you know?**

Salzburg means "salt city." Salzburg, Austria, got its name from the nearby salt mines. Money from the sale of salt let the city build grand churches and palaces.

9

3 What's Green and Growing in the Mountains

Different plants grow at different levels of a mountain. The plants are **adapted** to the temperatures and rainfall at each level.

Plants at low altitudes

Forests of **broad-leaved** trees, such as oaks and maples, grow at the bases of most mountains. In **temperate climates,** most of these trees are **deciduous.** Many other kinds of plants, such as wildflowers, ferns, and mosses grow in these forests.

In **tropical** climates, it is warm all year. Broad-leaved trees do not lose all their leaves at one time. Other plants, such as vines, orchids, and ferns grow in these forests.

The leaves of many deciduous trees, like these at the base of the Alps Mountains, change color in autumn. Then the leaves fall off the trees.

As it get colder and windier at high **altitudes,** trees have a harder time growing.

Plants at middle altitudes

Farther up the mountains, **coniferous** forests grow. Trees such as pine, fir, and spruce are **conifers.** They make seeds in cones and most have needlelike leaves. Most conifers are **evergreens.** They keep their leaves all year. Ferns, mosses, and wildflowers also grow in the coniferous forests. In the Alps, coniferous forests start at about 4,500 feet (1,370 meters). These forests stop growing at about 5,500 feet (1,675 meters).

The krummholz

If a mountain is tall enough, trees get smaller and farther apart near the top edge of the coniferous forest. The top edge is the krummholz, which means "crooked wood." Here you find clusters of dwarf trees that have been twisted by the strong, cold mountain winds.

Trumpet gentians grow in the alpine tundra in the Alps and Pyrenees of Europe. Other **species** of gentians grow on mountains in other parts of the world.

Plants at high altitudes

If a mountain is tall enough, it has a tree line. Above the tree line it is too cold and windy for trees to grow. In this area, **alpine tundra** plants grow. Alpine plants include grasses, mosses, and wildflowers. Lichens also grow here. But they are not plants. A lichen is a **fungus** and an **alga** that live together. Both gain from this living arrangement, which is called **mutualism.**

The snow line

Above a certain level, called the snow line, it is too cold for any plants to grow. Mountains in **tropical** regions that are taller than 15,000 feet (4,500 meters) have snow-capped peaks with no plants. Farther away from the **equator,** the snow line is lower. In the Alps, the snow line is about 9,000 feet (2,700 meters) high.

Plants also change with latitude

Plants that grow on mountains also change with **latitude.** This is the distance north or south of the equator. Many mountains of the Andes are located near the equator. Tropical plants such as palms and mahogany trees grow near the base of these mountains. Vines and orchids also grow in these tropical rain forests. In cold **climates** farther from the equator, such as in the Canadian Rockies, **coniferous** forests grow near the base of the mountains.

The farther north or south of the equator a mountain is, the lower the treeless alpine tundra begins. In warm tropical regions, trees can grow up to the 13,000-foot level (about 4,000 meters). But in the Alps, trees cannot grow above 5,500 feet (1,675 meters).

Tropical rain forest plants like these orchids grow at the bases of many mountains that are near the equator. Rain forests grow where rain falls throughout the year so the plants are never short of water.

4 What Animals Live in the Mountains?

Many different kinds of animals can live near the bases of mountains. But fewer animals can live high in the mountains.

Insects and spiders

Insects such as stoneflies and mayflies live in mountain streams. Beetles, grasshoppers, and butterflies live as high as the **alpine tundra.** Springtails and alpine wetas are small insects that live in cracks in the rocks above the snow line.

Spiders, both large and small, live in different life zones on mountains. Jumping spiders live high on Mount Everest in the Himalayas. They feed on flies and springtails.

Amphibians and reptiles

Few **amphibians** and **reptiles** can live in the cold temperatures high in mountains. These cold-blooded animals have body temperatures that change with their surroundings. Fire salamanders live in the mountains of Europe, Asia, and Africa. Giant salamanders live in the mountains of Japan. Short-horned lizards live in high mountain forests of western North America. Timber rattlesnakes live in the wooded Appalachians.

Japanese giant salamanders can be as long as 5 feet (1 1/2 meters).

Mountain bluebirds spend summers above 5,000 feet (1,525 meters) in the mountains of western North America. They feed on insects.

Birds

Many birds, such as hummingbirds and flycatchers, live near the bottoms of mountains. There they find plenty of seeds, fruits, flowers, and insects for food. American dippers live along clear, rushing mountain streams in North America. They will wade or even swim underwater to find food.

Steller's jays live high in **coniferous** forests of the Rocky Mountains. They feed on insects, berries, and seeds. Golden eagles live in high mountains in North America, Europe, and Asia. They glide above the land searching for small animals and birds. Andean condors soar over the Andes Mountains. They have one of the largest wingspans of any flying bird. Their wingspan is about 10 feet (3 meters). They can live as long as 72 years.

A snow leopard has broad, furry feet that help keep it from sinking into the snow on the high mountain slopes where it lives. It uses its long tail for balance when it leaps between rocks.

Mammals

Mammals of all sizes live in the mountains. Snow leopards live high in the Himalaya Mountains. They feed mainly on wild sheep and goats. Mountain lions live throughout mountains of North and South America. They feed mainly on deer.

Vicuñas are related to camels but they don't have humps. They live only in a few areas high in the Andes of South America. Small family groups feed on grasses and small plants. A male guards each herd. He whistles to warn of danger.

Heather voles are small mammals that live high in the mountains of North America. They live and nest on heather and grasses growing on the floor of **coniferous** forests.

How Do Animals Live in Mountains?

Some animals live in the same **life zone** of a mountain all the time. Others move up or down the mountain or leave in winter to find food.

Some animals move in winter

Deer and elk spend summers grazing in **alpine** meadows. They move down to valleys and forests to feed in winter. Black-necked cranes from Tibet are birds that move down the mountains in winter. Other birds **migrate** to mountains in summer but leave in winter. Dusky flycatchers nest in the Rocky Mountains. In winter they migrate to Mexico.

Some animals sleep through winter

Some mountain animals, such as ground squirrels, **hibernate** through cold winters. A hibernating animal goes into a deep sleep. To get ready for winter, it eats large amounts of food. It uses stored body fat as food. A **burrow** protects it from the cold.

Black-necked cranes nest in high-**altitude** marshes. They feed on such things as plant roots, snails, and small fish.

Some animals have heavy coats

Yaks, snow leopards, and vicuñas have thick coats that protect them during the cold winters. The fur grows in two layers. A soft, thick undercoat keeps an animal's body from losing heat. Long, slick outer hairs shed snow and keep out wind.

Some animals live in burrows or under rocks

Marmots are large relatives of ground squirrels. They live in family groups in **burrows.** Burrows give them a safe place to have young and to spend the cold winter. Pikas are small mammals related to rabbits. Groups of pikas live among rocks. If one spots an enemy, such as an eagle, it calls out a warning. Then they all dash into cracks in the rocks to hide.

Some animals store food

In mid-summer, pikas start piling up plants in rock shelters. The plants are their winter food. During winter, they travel in tunnels they dig under the snow.

A yak's long, shaggy hair reaches almost to the ground. In spring, it sheds its woolly undercoat.

18

What's for Dinner in the Mountains?

All living things need food. Some living things, like plants, can make their own food. But animals need to find and eat food to live.

Plants

Plants make, or produce, their own food. So they are called **producers.** To make food, plants use carbon dioxide gas from the air and water from the ground. Plants use energy from sunlight to change the carbon dioxide and water into sugars. This process of making food is called **photosynthesis. Broad-leaved** trees, **coniferous** trees, grasses, mosses, ferns, and wildflowers are all mountain producers.

Giant lobelias are producers that grow high in the mountains of Africa. These plants grow for about 20 years, then flower once, and die.

❓ Did you know?

Algae belong to a group of living things called **protists.** In lichens, the algae are producers. They make food for themselves and the **fungi** they live with.

Animals

Animals are called **consumers** because they eat, or consume, food. Some mountain animals, such as yaks, wild sheep, and pikas, eat only plants. These animals are called **herbivores.** Other animals, such as red pandas, ground squirrels, and snow finches, eat both plants and animals. They are **omnivores.** Still others, such as golden eagles, lynxes, and snow leopards, eat only animals. They are **carnivores.**

Mountain goats are herbivores. They feed on mosses and other vegetation found above the tree line in the Rocky Mountains. Rough pads on the bottom of their hooves help them grip the steep ground.

The clean-up crew

Decomposers feed on dead plants and animals and their wastes. **Bacteria, molds,** and some beetles are decomposers. Decomposers break down **nutrients** stored in dead plants and animals. They put them back into the soil, air, and water. Plants use the nutrients to help them grow.

Some mountain animals hunt for food. Others **forage** or **scavenge** for food.

Hunting

Animals that hunt and kill other animals for food are **predators.** Golden eagles are predators. The hunt and eat small **mammals,** snakes, and other birds. Lynxes chase down and eat hares and ground squirrels. So they are predators. Ground squirrels eat plants. But they also hunt and eat insects. So sometimes they are predators. Animals that predators eat are called **prey.** Hares are prey of lynxes and golden eagles. Insects are prey of ground squirrels.

Golden eagles are swift predators. They can snatch a bird out of the air or lift a running rabbit off the ground in an instant.

Some mountain animals are both predators and prey. Mountain chickadees are small birds that eat insects and caterpillars. So, they are predators. However, chickadees are also eaten by golden eagles and owls. So, they are also prey.

Other scavengers often feed on the bodies of dead animals before the bearded vulture eats. It is often left with just the bones.

Foraging

Some animals, such as elk, mountain goats, yaks, vicuñas, and giant pandas, are **foragers.** They move about from place to place, sometimes in groups, to search for food. They search for grasses, buds, leaves, twigs, and lichens to eat.

Scavenging

Some mountain animals are **scavengers.** Scavengers are animals that eat the bodies of animals or plants that are already dead. Andean condors and bearded vultures are scavengers.

Bearded vultures carry bones from dead animals high into the air and drop the bones onto the rocks below. When the bones break open, they can eat the soft marrow inside.

? Did you know?

There are fewer than a thousand giant pandas left in the mountains of China.

Planning the menu

The path that shows who eats what is a **food chain.** All living things are parts of food chains. In the **alpine tundra** of mountains in Europe, mountain hares eat alpine grasses and flowers. Golden eagles eat hares.

Another alpine tundra food chain includes snowy voles that eat grasses. The voles are eaten by lynxes. A third food chain includes ibexes that also eat grasses. Young ibexes are eaten by golden eagles. Vultures, who are scavengers, feed on all the animals in the **habitat** that die. All the food chains that are connected in a habitat make up a **food web.** Many living things in a food web are part of more than one food chain.

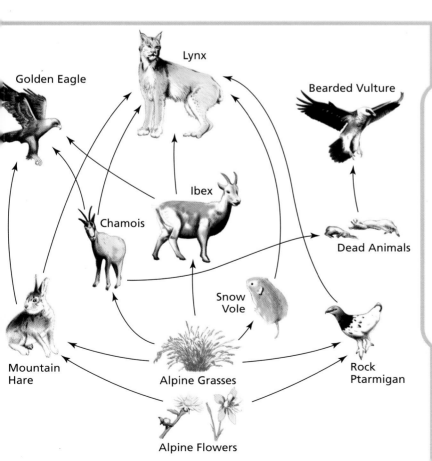

Golden Eagle
Lynx
Bearded Vulture
Ibex
Chamois
Dead Animals
Snow Vole
Mountain Hare
Alpine Grasses
Rock Ptarmigan
Alpine Flowers

In a food web, an arrow is drawn from "dinner" and points to the "diner." So, producers are on the bottom of the web. "Top" predators, animals that no one else eats, are at the top.

How Do Mountains Affect People?

Mountains can be difficult and dangerous places for people to live. And they can even affect people who don't live in them.

Mountains collect water

Tall mountains store water on their snowy peaks. Melting snow forms rivers that flow into the valleys below. The rivers give people water for drinking, cleaning, and growing crops.

Mountains have landslides and avalanches

Mountains sometimes change in only a few minutes. Heavy rain or a small earthquake can cause a **landslide.** Rocks and soil suddenly crash down the mountainside. A big landslide destroys everything in its path. Large blocks of snow also can break loose. Then, an **avalanche** comes roaring down the mountain. An avalanche can travel as fast as 200 miles (322 kilometers) an hour.

Pine forests high on mountains can often hold back avalanches. In places where the mountain slopes aren't covered by forests, avalanches can destroy whole towns.

Walls of mud 130 feet (40 meters) high swept down valleys below the Nevado del Ruiz volcano, destroying towns.

Volcanic mountains erupt

Living near volcanic mountains can be dangerous. In 1902, Mount Pelée on the Caribbean island of Martinique erupted. Hot gases and ash raced down the mountain. A town at its base was destroyed. More than 30,000 people were killed.

On November 13, 1985, Colombia's Nevado del Ruiz volcano erupted. Heat from the volcano melted snow on the mountain. Melted snow mixed with soil and formed huge mudflows. Nearly 23,000 people died.

Living at high altitudes

High in mountains, the air is thinner and there is not as much oxygen in it. Native people who live high in the Andes are **adapted** to the thin air. They have larger lungs that allow them to take in more air with each breath. Their blood has more red blood cells to carry oxygen to all parts of their bodies.

9 How Do People Affect Mountains?

Few people live in mountains. But many people use mountains and their **resources.**

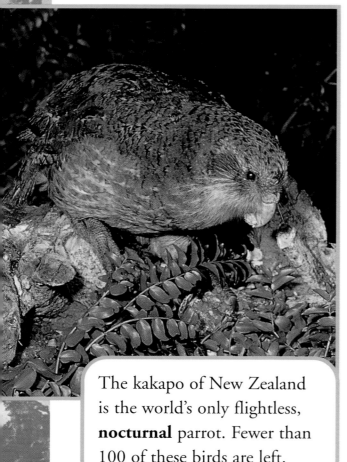

The kakapo of New Zealand is the world's only flightless, **nocturnal** parrot. Fewer than 100 of these birds are left.

People damage habitats

In many places, mountain forests have been cut down. Animals have lost food and shelter. Without tree roots to hold soil in place, the soil washes away. Flooding, avalanches, and landslides happen more often.

People also mine **minerals** in mountains. **Pollution** from mining harms water and land.

When New Zealand was settled, people brought in **predators,** such as pet cats. These predators have caused some flightless mountain birds to become **extinct** or **endangered.**

People hunt animals

Many mountain animals are endangered and are protected by laws. Rangers try to protect them. But **poachers** sometimes kill them anyway. Snow leopards are killed for their fur. Mountain gorillas live in mountains of Rwanda and Uganda in Africa. Poachers sell their body parts.

The Appalachian National Scenic Trail passes through 14 states, two national parks, and eight national forests. It follows the crests of mountains from Mt. Katahdin in Maine to Springer Mountain in Georgia.

People use mountains for recreation

People hike in mountains like the Appalachians. They also climb high mountains like the Himalayas. Mountain climbers leave trash in Himalayas because it takes too much energy to bring it back down the mountain. Some people climb up just to collect the trash. People also build ski resorts in mountains. Ski resorts can destroy mountain **habitats.**

People protect mountains

Many parks and nature reserves have been created to protect mountain habitats. Swiss National Park protects animals like chamois and ibexes. It also protects edelweiss plants. Other parks in the Alps protect golden eagles. Fiordland National Park in New Zealand protects many species of mountain plants and animals. Mountains are beautiful places. People must protect them and use them carefully.

Fact File

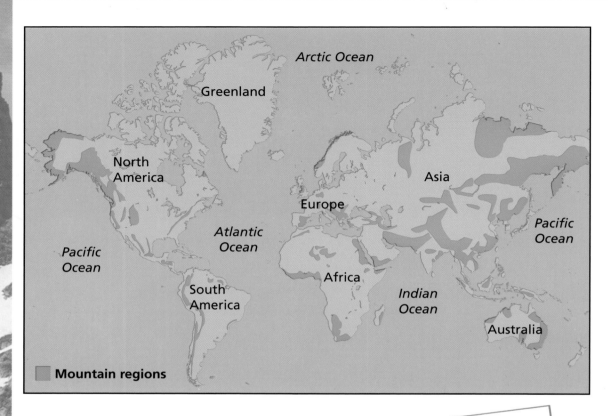

Mountain regions

Year of the Mountain
The year 2002 was declared the International Year of the Mountain by the United Nations. Programs were established to "improve the lives of mountain people, protect fragile mountain ecosystems, and promote peace and stability in mountain regions."
About 770 million people live in mountain regions. About 50 million people visit mountains each year. In the Alps, the Andes, the Himalayas, and the Rockie Mountains, as much as 90 percent of the local people's income is from mountain tourism.

Earth's Mountains

Mountain	Location	Facts
Alaska Range	south central Alaska	Mount McKinley, also called Denali, (20,320 ft*/ 6,194 m**) is the highest point in North America.
Alps	central Europe	The youngest of Earth's great mountain ranges; Mont Blanc (14,771 ft/4,807 m) is the tallest peak; the Alps in France, Austria, Switzerland, and Italy have the most deadly avalanches every year.
Altai Mountains	Western Mongolia and Kazakstan in Asia	Contain rich deposits of lead, zinc, gold, silver, copper, and iron; Belukha (14,783 ft/4,506 m) is the tallest peak.
Andes	western South America	The longest mountain range on Earth—stretching 4,500 miles (7,200 km); Aconcagua (22,840 ft/6,960 m) is the tallest peak.
Appalachians	eastern United States	The oldest mountains in North America; Mount Mitchell (6,684 ft/2,037 m) is the tallest peak.
Atlas Mountains	northwestern Africa	Jebel Toubkal (13,665 ft/4,165 m) is the tallest peak.
Cascade Range	along the coast of Washington, Oregon and northern California	Contains many snowcapped volcanic mountains, including Mount St. Helens; Mount Rainier (14,410 ft/ 4,392 m) is the tallest peak.
Drakensberg Mountains	South Africa	Injasuti (11,181 ft/3,408 m) is the tallest peak.
Great Dividing Range/ Australian Alps	eastern Australia	Mount Kosciusko (7,310 ft/2,228 m) is the tallest peak; it and other tall peaks are snow covered in winter.
Himalayas	Asia, beginning at the northern edge of India.	The highest mountain range on Earth; Mount Everest (29,108 ft/8,872 m) is the world's highest mountain.
Pyrenees	between France and Spain	Pico de Aneto (11,168 ft/3,404 m), in Spain, is the tallest peak.
Rocky Mountains	western North America (United States and Canada)	Mount Elbert (14,432 ft/4,399 m) in Colorado is the tallest peak; in the United States, Colorado, Alaska, and Utah have the most deadly avalanches.
Southern Alps	South Island, New Zealand	Mount Cook (12,349 ft/3,764 m) is the tallest peak.
Ural Mountains	between Europe and Asia	Toward the Arctic the mountains are covered with tundra plants; farther south some conifers grow; Mount Narodnaya (6,214 ft/1,894 m) is the tallest peak.

*ft = feet
**m =meters

Glossary

adapted changed to live under certain conditions

alga (plural: algae) a producer that lives in damp places

alpine living on mountains above the tree line

altitude how high a place is above the ocean or sea level

amphibian animal with a moist skin that lives on land but lays its eggs in water. Frogs, toads, and salamanders are amphibians.

avalanche large mass of snow and ice loosened from a mountainside that swiftly moves down the mountain

bacteria living things too small to be seen except with a microscope. Some bacteria are decomposers.

biodiversity variety of life, or number of different species, in a habitat

broad-leaved having wide, flat leaves

burrow hole dug in the ground by animals for shelter

carnivore animal that eats only other animals

climate average weather conditions in an area over a long period of time

conifer trees that make their seeds in cones

coniferous making seeds in cones

consumer living thing that needs plants for food

deciduous shedding leaves at a particular season

decomposer consumer that puts nutrients from dead plants and animals back into the soil, air, and water.

endangered likely to become extinct. Kakapos and snow leopards are endangered animals.

equator imaginary circle around Earth halfway between the North Pole and the South Pole

erosion moving of soil and rocks by water, wind, or ice

evergreen having green leaves or needles all year long

extinct no longer existing on Earth

food chain path that shows who eats what in a habitat

food web group of connected food chains in a habitat

forage wander about in search of food

forager animal or person that wanders about searching for food

fungus (plural: fungi) living thing that feeds on dead or living plant or animal matter. Mushrooms and molds are fungi.

habitat place where a plant or animal naturally lives

herbivore animal that eats only plants

hibernate spend the winter in a state in which an animal's breathing, heart rate, and body temperature is greatly reduced

landslide mass of rock and soil sliding down a steep slope

latitude distance north or south of the equator

life zone habitat found at a particular altitude on a mountain

mammal warm-blooded animal that breathes with lungs, has a bony skeleton, has hair or fur, and produces milk to feed its young

migrate move from one place to another with the change of seasons

mineral any material dug from the earth by mining. Gold, iron, and diamonds are minerals.

mold living thing that uses dead plants and animals for food. Molds are decomposers.

mutualism relationship between two species that helps both living things

nocturnal active at night

nutrient material that is needed for the growth of a plant or animal

omnivore animal that eats plants and animals

photosynthesis process by which green plants trap the sun's energy and use it to change carbon dioxide and water into sugars

poacher person who kills animals that are protected by law

pollution harmful materials in the water, air, or land

predator animal that hunts and eats other animals

prey animal that is hunted and eaten by other animals

producer living thing that can use sunlight to make its own food

protist type of living thing that is neither a plant nor an animal. Algae are protists.

range group of mountains

reptile land animal with a scaly skin. Snakes, lizards, turtles, and crocodiles are reptiles.

resource anything that meets a need that people, plants, or animals have

scavenge feed on the bodies of dead animals

scavenger animal that eats the bodies of animals that are already dead

species group of living things that are enough alike that they can mate and reproduce

temperate has warm or hot summers and cool or cold winters

tropical region near the equator that is warm to hot all year round

tundra cold, treeless area

More Books to Read

Bograd, Larry. *The Rocky Mountains*. New York: Benchmark Books, 2000.

Fowler, Allan. *Living in the Mountains*. Danbury, Conn.: Children's Press, 2000.

Gray, Susan Heinrichs. *Mountains*. Mankato, Minn.: Compass Point Books, 2000.

Green, Jen. *People of the Mountains*. Austin, Tex.: Raintree Steck-Vaughn, 1998.

Index